THE LIFE OF HARRIET TUBMAN

BY ELIZABETH RAUM

SEQUENCE

AMICUS AMICUS INK

Sequence is published by Amicus and Amicus Ink
P.O. Box 227, Mankato, MN 56002
www.amicuspublishing.us

Library of Congress Cataloging-in-Publication Data
Names: Raum, Elizabeth, author.
Title: The life of Harriet Tubman / by Elizabeth Raum.
Description: Mankato, Minnesota : Amicus, [2020] | Series: Sequence change maker biographies | Includes index. | Audience: Grades K-3.
Identifiers: LCCN 2018032016 (print) | LCCN 2018032375 (ebook) | ISBN 9781681517582 (pdf) | ISBN 9781681516769 (library binding) | ISBN 9781681524627 (pbk.)
Subjects: LCSH: Tubman, Harriet, 1822-1913. | Slaves--United States--Biography--Juvenile literature. | African American women--Biography--Juvenile literature. | Underground Railroad--Juvenile literature. | Fugitive slaves--United States--History--19th century--Juvenile literature. | Antislavery movements--United States--History--19th century--Juvenile literature.
Classification: LCC E444.T82 (ebook) | LCC E444.T82 R37 2020 (print) | DDC 306.3/62092 [B]--dc23
LC record available at https://lccn.loc.gov/2018032016

Editor: Alissa Thielges
Designer: Ciara Beitlich
Photo Researcher: Holly Young

Photo Credits: Library of Congress/Benjamin F. Powelson cover; WikiCommons/Henry P. Moore cover, 16; LOC/Lindsley, Harvey B. 4; WikiCommons/Unknown artist 7; Getty/Kean Collection 8; Getty/Print Collector 11, 12, 28–29; WikiCommons/Sarah H Bradford 11; Alamy/Walter Oleksy 12; WikiCommons/Cambridge Democrat 12; WikiCommons/Charles T. Webber 14–15; LOC 16; Alamy/Maurice Savage 19; Getty/Bettmann 19; Alamy/National Geographic Image Collection 20; LOC/Kurz and Allison 23; WikiCommons/McPherson & Oliver 24; Alamy/Vespasian 27; Alamy/Randy Duchaine 28

TABLE OF CONTENTS

As an escaped slave, Harriet helped many others to freedom.

LOADING... LOADING... LOADING...

Who was Harriet Tubman?

In the mid-1800s, Harriet Tubman helped dozens of people escape from **slavery**. She guided them along the **Underground Railroad**. This was a hidden route from southern states to northern states. During the Civil War (1861–1865), she served as a nurse and a spy. She even led a **raid**. She was the first woman to do so.

LOADING . . . LOADING . . . LOADING . . .

Life Under Slavery

Harriet Tubman was born in Maryland around 1820. Her birthday is not known. As a slave, her birth was not recorded. Her parents, Harriet Green and Benjamin Ross, named her Araminta. They called her "Minty." Like her family, Minty was born into slavery. She lived in fear of being separated from her family.

Harriet Tubman is born.

ABOUT 1820

LOADING . . . LOADING . . .

Slaves, like Minty's family, were seen as property. They were sold and traded in auctions.

LOADING... LOADING... LOADING...

Harriet Tubman is born.

ABOUT 1820 ABOUT 1835 ...ING . . . LOADING . . .

Harriet suffers head injury.

At age five, Minty was sent to a nearby farm. There, she babysat. If the baby cried, Minty was beaten. She was often hungry and ill. When she was about 15, she tried to help a runaway slave. She was hit in the head with a heavy weight. She nearly died. For the rest of her life, she suffered headaches and sleeping spells.

Running away was dangerous. A slave risks his life to be free.

LOADING... LOADING... LOADING...

Minty was only five feet tall. But hard work made her strong. She was happy outdoors. She never went to school. She didn't know how to read or write. In 1844, she married John Tubman. She called herself Harriet after her mother. John was a **freeman**. Harriet was not.

As a slave, Harriet cooked and cleaned inside. Outside, she worked in the field and cut wood.

ABOUT 1820	ABOUT 1835	1844
Harriet Tubman is born.	Harriet suffers head injury.	Harriet marries John Tubman.

. . . LOADING . . .

LOADING . . . LOADING . . . LOADING . . .

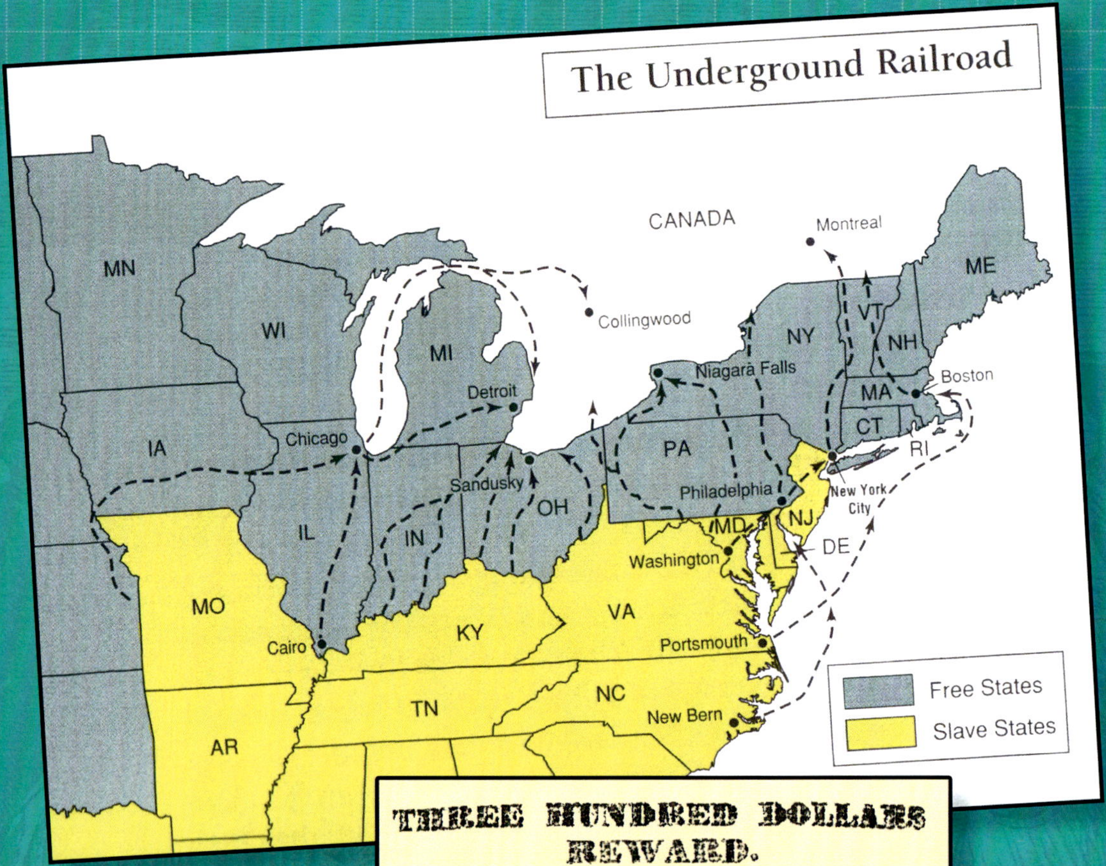

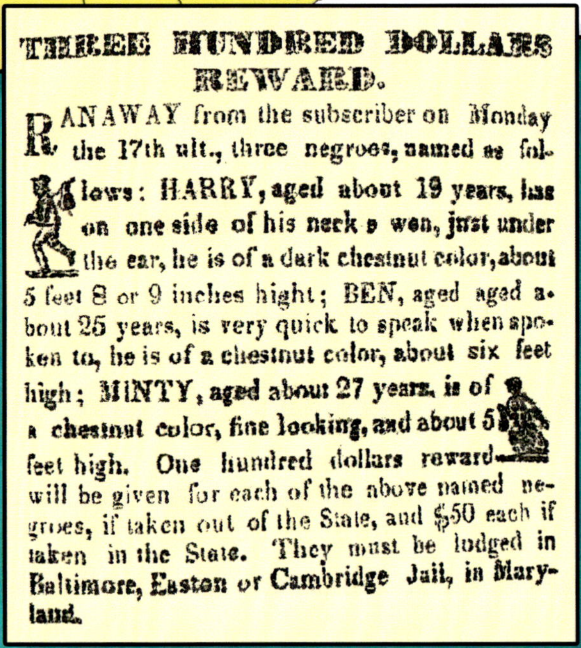

THREE HUNDRED DOLLARS REWARD.

RANAWAY from the subscriber on Monday the 17th ult., three negroes, named as follows: HARRY, aged about 19 years, has on one side of his neck a wen, just under the ear, he is of a dark chestnut color, about 5 feet 8 or 9 inches hight; BEN, aged aged about 25 years, is very quick to speak when spoken to, he is of a chestnut color, about six feet high; MINTY, aged about 27 years, is of a chestnut color, fine looking, and about 5 feet high. One hundred dollars reward will be given for each of the above named negroes, if taken out of the State, and $50 each if taken in the State. They must be lodged in Baltimore, Easton or Cambridge Jail, in Maryland.

ABOUT 1820	ABOUT 1835	1844	1849
Harriet Tubman is born.	Harriet suffers head injury.	Harriet marries John Tubman.	Harriet escapes slavery; takes Underground Railroad to freedom.

READING . . .

Escaping Slavery

In 1849, Harriet's master died. The new owner was going to sell all his slaves. Harriet planned to escape. John refused to go. Harriet left with two of her brothers. But her brothers got scared. They turned back. Harriet went on alone. She traveled on the Underground Railroad. This was a secret **network** of people who helped runaway slaves.

The map shows routes slaves took to the north. Below is the reward offered for Harriet's capture.

LOADING . . . LOADING . . . LOADING . . .

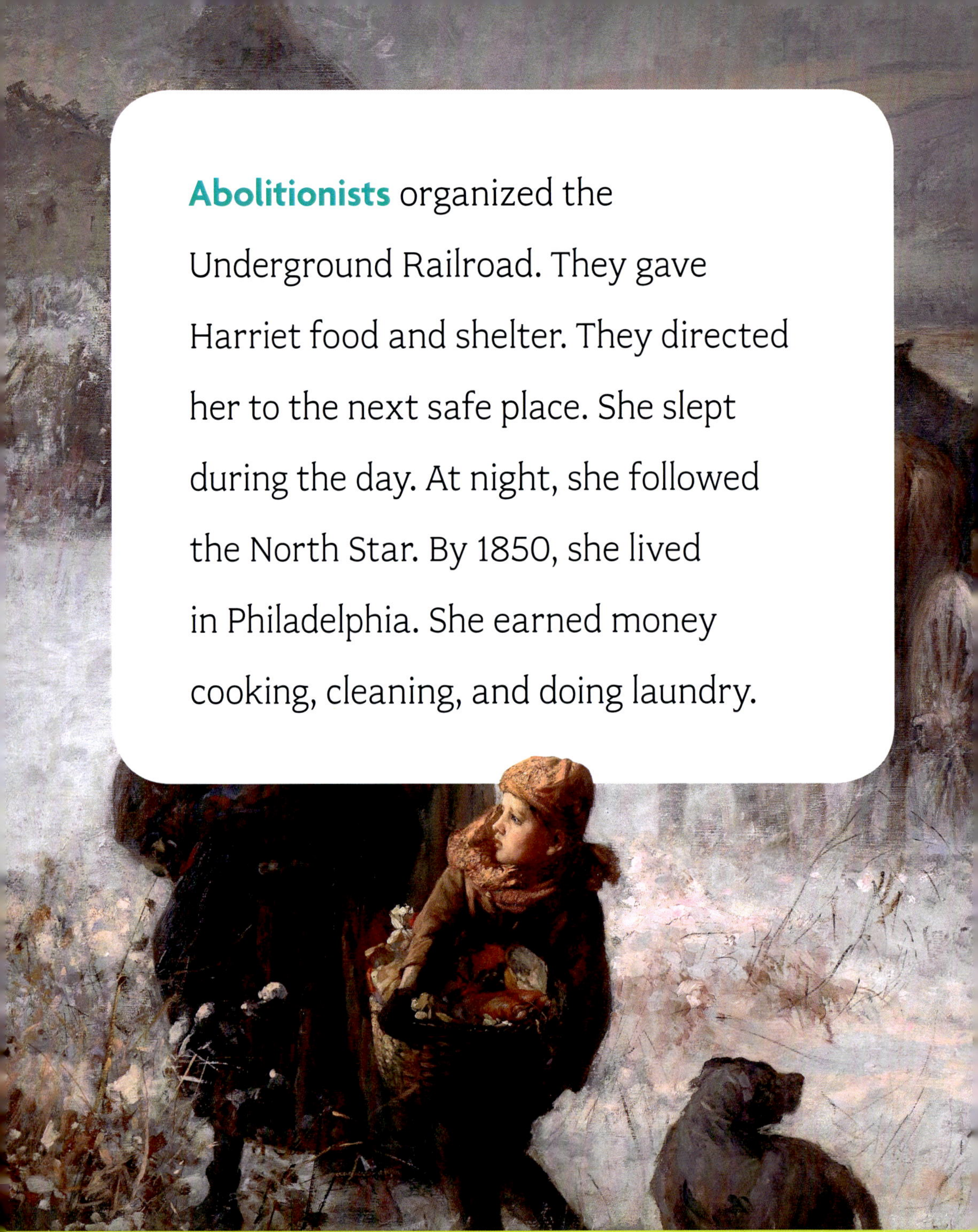

Abolitionists organized the Underground Railroad. They gave Harriet food and shelter. They directed her to the next safe place. She slept during the day. At night, she followed the North Star. By 1850, she lived in Philadelphia. She earned money cooking, cleaning, and doing laundry.

- ABOUT 1820: Harriet Tubman is born.
- ABOUT 1835: Harriet suffers head injury.
- 1844: Harriet marries John Tubman.
- 1849: Harriet escapes slavery; takes Underground Railroad to freedom.
- 1850: **Harriet works in Philadelphia.**

People along the Underground Railroad helped slaves get to freedom.

LOADING . . . LOADING . . . LOADING . . .

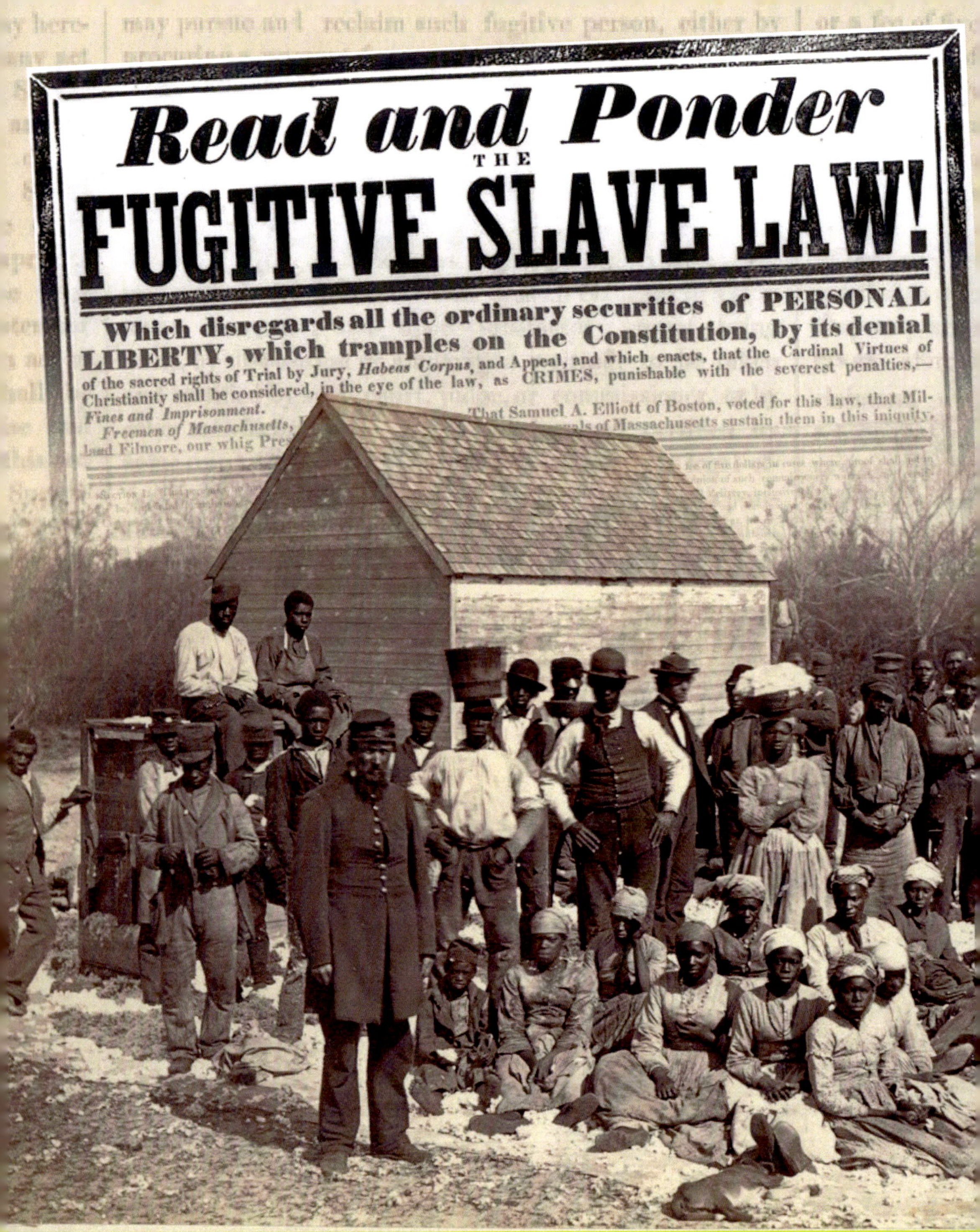

- ABOUT 1820 — Harriet Tubman is born.
- ABOUT 1835 — Harriet suffers head injury.
- 1844 — Harriet marries John Tubman.
- 1849 — Harriet escapes slavery; takes Underground Railroad to freedom.
- 1850 — Harriet works in Philadelphia.
- **Congress passes the Fugitive Slave Law.**

On September 18, 1850, Congress passed the **Fugitive** Slave Law. This law punished those who helped runaway slaves. Philadelphia was no longer safe. No state was. Harriet fled to Canada. The Underground Railroad led there, too. Slavery was against the law in Canada.

The new law made life harder for slaves. Some, like these people, wouldn't be freed until the Civil War.

Harriet wanted to free her family. She learned that her niece, Kessiah, was about to be sold. Before the sale, Kessiah and her family ran away. They hid in a wagon and then a boat. Harriet met them in Baltimore, Maryland. In December 1850, she took them to Canada.

Runaway slaves hide in a wagon to travel north. An ad announced the sale of Kessiah.

ABOUT 1820	Harriet Tubman is born.
ABOUT 1835	Harriet suffers head injury.
1844	Harriet marries John Tubman.
1849	Harriet escapes slavery; takes Underground Railroad to freedom.
1850	Harriet works in Philadelphia.
	Congress passes the Fugitive Slave Law.

NEGRO FOR SALE.

I WILL sell at public sale to the highest bidder for cash, at the Court house door in the town of Cambridge, on MONDAY the 10th day of September next, a negro woman named KIZZIAH, aged about 25 years. She will be sold for life, and a good title will be given. Attendance given by

JOHN MILLS,
Agent for Elizabeth Brodess.

Harriet rescues her niece.

LOADING . . . LOADING . . .

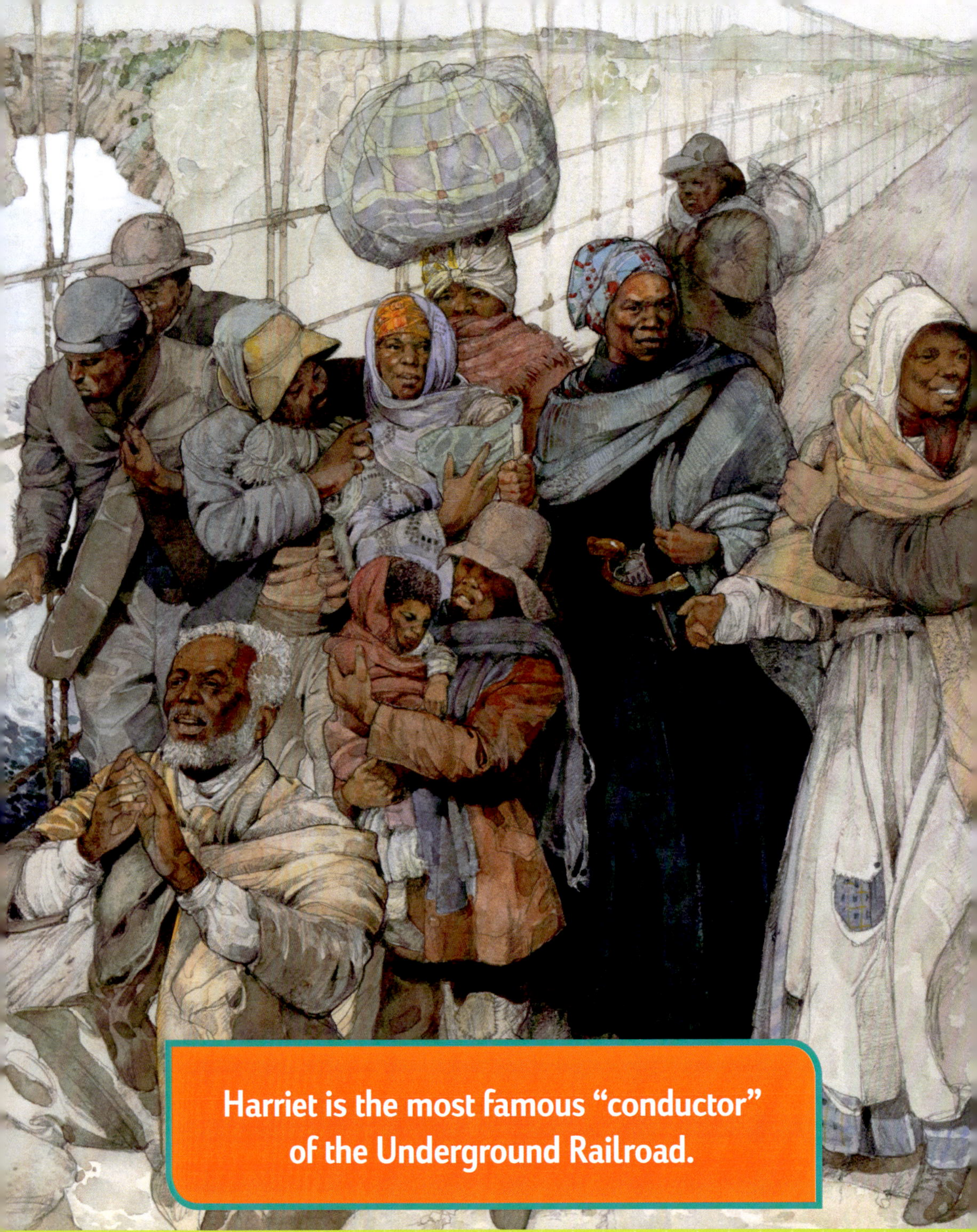

Harriet is the most famous "conductor" of the Underground Railroad.

- ABOUT 1820 — Harriet Tubman is born.
- ABOUT 1835 — Harriet suffers head injury.
- 1844 — Harriet marries John Tubman.
- 1849 — Harriet escapes slavery; takes Underground Railroad to freedom.
- 1850 — Harriet works in Philadelphia.
- Congress passes the Fugitive Slave Law.

Between 1851 and 1860, Harriet made at least 13 trips to Maryland. She led dozens of people to Canada. She never lost a single "passenger." Slave owners heard what she was doing. They offered a reward for Harriet's capture or death. She used different routes to avoid capture. She was never once caught.

Harriet rescues her niece.

1851 – 1860

Harriet makes at least 13 Underground Railroad trips.

...DING . . . LOADING . . .

Working to End Slavery

In April 1861, the Civil War began. Harriet bought a house in Auburn, N.Y. She was safe there, but she wanted to help end slavery. The **Union** Army opposed slavery. Harriet joined them as a nurse. She worked in Virginia and later in South Carolina. She formed a group of spies on the Carolina coast. It was made up of local enslaved men.

ABOUT 1820	Harriet Tubman is born.
ABOUT 1835	Harriet suffers head injury.
1844	Harriet marries John Tubman.
1849	Harriet escapes slavery; takes Underground Railroad to freedom.
1850	Harriet works in Philadelphia.
1850	Congress passes the Fugitive Slave Law.

Many black men fought with the Union Army in the Civil War.

Harriet rescues her niece.

1851 – 1860

Harriet makes at least 13 Underground Railroad trips.

1861

Civil War begins; Harriet works as nurse and spy for Union Army.

...LOADING...

Harriet Tubman is born.
ABOUT 1820

Harriet suffers head injury.
ABOUT 1835

Harriet marries John Tubman.
1844

Harriet escapes slavery; takes Underground Railroad to freedom.
1849

Harriet works in Philadelphia.
1850

Congress passes the Fugitive Slave Law.

On June 2, 1863, Harriet led 150 African-American soldiers on the Combahee River Raid. Fugitive slaves were hiding along the South Carolina River. Harriet sang to encourage them to get into Union boats. More than 700 slaves were **liberated** that day. Harriet was the first woman to lead U.S. troops in military action.

Slaves swim out to the boats in the Combahee River Raid.

Harriet rescues her niece.

1851 – 1860: Harriet makes at least 13 Underground Railroad trips.

1861: Civil War begins; Harriet works as nurse and spy for Union Army.

1863: Harriet is the first woman to lead U.S. troops.

Life After the Civil War

In 1864, Harriet returned to her home in Auburn, New York. After the war, she raised money for African-American schools in North Carolina. She also joined the fight for women's **suffrage**. In 1896, she opened the Harriet Tubman Home for the Aged in Auburn.

- ABOUT 1820: Harriet Tubman is born.
- ABOUT 1835: Harriet suffers head injury.
- 1844: Harriet marries John Tubman.
- 1849: Harriet escapes slavery; takes Underground Railroad to freedom.
- 1850: Harriet works in Philadelphia.
- Congress passes the Fugitive Slave Law.

Harriet's Home for the Aged was built on her land. It is now a museum.

Harriet rescues her niece.

1851 – 1860: Harriet makes at least 13 Underground Railroad trips.

1861: Civil War begins; Harriet works as nurse and spy for Union Army.

1863: Harriet is the first woman to lead U.S. troops.

1896: Harriet opens a home for the elderly.

Harriet Tubman is born.

ABOUT 1820

Harriet suffers head injury.

ABOUT 1835

Harriet marries John Tubman.

1844

Harriet escapes slavery; takes Underground Railroad to freedom.

1849

Harriet works in Philadelphia.

1850

Congress passes the Fugitive Slave Law.

In 1913, Harriet died. She was about 93. She was buried with military honors. In 1978, she was the first African-American woman to have her face on a U.S. stamp. In 2014, the Harriet Tubman Underground Railroad National Historical Park opened in Maryland. At the time, President Barack Obama called Harriet Tubman "an American hero."

This statue shows Harriet leading people to freedom. It is in Boston, Massachusetts.

- Harriet rescues her niece.
- 1851 – 1860: Harriet makes at least 13 Underground Railroad trips.
- 1861: Civil War begins; Harriet works as nurse and spy for Union Army.
- 1863: Harriet is the first woman to lead U.S. troops.
- 1896: Harriet opens a home for the elderly.
- 1913: Harriet dies at age 93.

Glossary

abolitionist A person who worked to abolish, or eliminate, slavery.

freeman A person who is free.

fugitive A person who is running away from the law or a difficult situation.

liberate To free someone or be set free.

network A system of people that are connected through a common cause.

raid A sudden, surprise attack on an enemy or in enemy territory.

slavery The practice of owning people as property, forcing them work and obey.

suffrage The right to vote.

Underground Railroad A network of people who provided food, shelter, and transportation to people trying to escape slavery.

Union The states that remained loyal to the federal government; the North.

Read More

Barton, Jen. *What's Your Story, Harriet Tubman?* Minneapolis: Lerner, 2016.

Cline-Ransome, Lesa. *Before She Was Harriet.* New York: Holiday House, 2017.

Meltzer, Brad. *I Am Harriet Tubman.* New York: Dial, 2018.

Troupe, Thomas Kingsley. *Harriet Tubman's Escape.* North Mankato, Minn.: Picture Window Books, 2017.

Websites

Harriet Tubman Underground Railroad National Historic Park
https://www.nps.gov/hatu/index.htm

Meet Amazing Americans: Harriet Tubman
http://www.americaslibrary.gov/aa/tubman/aa_tubman_subj.html

PBS Explore | Harriet Tubman
http://www.pbs.org/black-culture/explore/harriet-tubman/#.XAVqHxNKhR5

Index

About the Author

Elizabeth Raum has written over 100 books for young readers. Many are biographies. She enjoys learning about people who help us see the world in new and exciting ways. She lives in Fargo, North Dakota. To learn more, visit her website: www.ElizabethRaumBooks.com.